Guide to

Reopening a Business

Following

Worldwide COVID -19 (Corona Virus)
Pandemic

Or an emergency closure from fire, storm,
flooding, etc.

Richard Larkin, M.B.A., Ed.D.

ISBN:

Table of Contents

Introduction

During 2020 the COVID-19 pandemic, the government mandated closure of most schools and businesses in the United States so quickly that many owners were caught unprepared. Nearly all businesses in the United States had to lock their doors, keep customers away; and people throughout the nation were told to stay in their homes. The government closed the country with almost no information about how long schools and businesses would be closed, or what to expect when they were going to be able to reopen, if ever.

Most small business owners were not ready for a closure. Their normal focus is on staying open and helping their company grow. When the emergency closure occurred, many business owners were faced with two questions:

1. what should they do to ensure the health and safety of their employees and their customers when they reopen?

2. how can they get former customers to return and how can they attract new customers?

These two questions generated the desire to write this *Guide* to help small business owners develop an orderly plan to reopen their company when they have permission to do so.

While researching to write a "reopening" guide, the author realized that the urgency of the business closure might have caused a lot of confusion related to *closing* a business. As a result, it is **_written in four parts with the third addressing how to reopen a business_**.

The first two parts of the *Guide* suggest steps a company should take while they quickly close business operations and how to operate a business which has been designated as "essential" during a nationwide closure.

The last part of the *Guide* shares some ideas on how a business owner can work with the community to help rebuild businesses.

Definitions

Pandemic

An outbreak of a disease that spreads and affects a significant portion of a population across a wide geographic area very quickly.

New normal

Previously unfamiliar business processes and customer relationships that are becoming standard, or usual and expected following the dramatic changes caused by the Pandemic and nationwide business closures of 2020.

"New normal" means adapting business practices to deal with current situations rather than expending energy on what business functions were like in the past.

Social distancing

According to public health officials, social distancing refers to deliberately increasing the physical space between people to avoid spreading illness.

Think of social distance (about six feet) as the length of space from hand to hand for an adult with their arms spread out on each side

Part one – Closing a Business

Chapter 1   Emergency preparedness

No business other than emergency services (first responders) and some government organizations expect an emergency or disaster to affect them, their employees, their customers, their facility, and their business without warning.

Many small businesses try to remain aware of health and safety risks to their daily operations but very few maintain a workplace emergency action plan, or train their employees to shut down critical operations, operate fire extinguishers, and help customers exit safely.

The United States Department of Labor has a helpful booklet on the Internet which can be found using the search terms "how to plan for workplace emergencies and evacuations." It is provided by OSHA (Occupational Safety and Health Act) and as a public domain publication, can be "...reproduced fully or partially without permission."

Chapter 2   Emergency action plan

According to OSHA, a company emergency action plan should include, at a minimum:

- a clear and well understood method for reporting fires and other emergencies
- emergency evacuation procedures including workplace maps and safe gathering locations identified for employees and customers
- assignments for employees who are responsible for accounting for all individuals present in a specific workplace at the time of an emergency
- names, titles, departments, and contact numbers of individuals both inside and outside the company to contact for additional information and direction (include company management, accountant, legal advisor)
- procedures for employees who remain to perform or shut down critical operations (equipment), operate fire suppression and security systems, or perform essential services that cannot be shut down for every emergency alarm before evacuating
- a regularly updated training record showing all employees and staff members of the company are familiar with the emergency action plan and have attended basic first aid courses

Chapter 3   Government emergency business closure

Normal business closures are planned over a period of months by addressing how to protect ownership assets, credit ratings, the company reputation with employees, lenders, and customers.

In the case of the **coronavirus (COVID-19) pandemic,** most small businesses were forced to close quickly with no time to develop a *closing plan*. As a result of the quick, unplanned government mandate, many small business owners were left not knowing whether their closure would be permanent or temporary and, if temporary, how long until they would be able to open.

Chapter 4   **Steps to close a business**

Businesses facing an immediate closure due to government direction or a disaster such as a fire or major storm might not have the luxury of "time" to prepare. Immediate or emergent business closures should attempt to follow the following steps:

Emergent or quick business closure:

- notify utilities, service or maintenance providers, suppliers, other creditors
- notify customers and coordinate settlement of outstanding open orders or partial payments received
- notify landlord and adjust lease agreement
- notify and pay employees
- contact a business law attorney to assist with the closure activities and help prepare for a reopening of the business
- notify insurance carrier
- liquidate perishable, but salvageable inventory
- pay existing debts if possible
- pay federal, state, and local taxes and payroll fees
- submit sales tax forms and funds up to date of closure
- provide contact information to business contacts, creditors, and employees

Long-term closure or a going out of business shutdown should follow these steps:

- contact a business law attorney to assist with the closure process
- collect accounts receivable
- sell inventory (consider a going out of business sale)
- notify utilities, service or maintenance providers, suppliers, other creditors
- notify customers and coordinate settlement of outstanding open orders or partial payments received
- notify landlord and adjust to a business closure lease agreement
- notify and pay employees
- notify insurance carrier
- liquidate perishable, but salvageable inventory
- pay existing debts if possible
- pay federal, state, and local taxes and payroll fees
- submit sales tax forms and funds up to date of closure
- cancel business credit accounts, maintenance contracts, and related ongoing business agreements

- close business bank accounts – a new one might be required to handle late accounts receivable payments and business closure expenses
- cancel business licenses and agreements
- file final employment and income tax forms
- provide contact information to business contacts, creditors, and employees

Part two

Operating during Pandemic

Chapter 5 – Operating during a pandemic

Businesses which are designated as *critical* and allowed to operate during a government closure will still have to make some changes to their daily operations. Whether the business is a repair facility, a grocery store, a health provider, or part of any other type of *critical* industry, they will have to minimize person-to-person contact and monitor the health of people inside their facility.

Any business continuing to operate during a mandated *closure* period must put employee and customer safety as their number oner priority.

Businesses operating during a pandemic should protect employees and customers by providing little or no contact between individuals. They can accomplish this by offering on-line service requests with in-car drop off and pick up for customers, credit/debit card payment processing with no hand to hand contact, product delivery with social distancing, and plexiglass screening for across counter transactions.

Some businesses are considered critical during a pandemic (e.g. health providers, grocery stores, defense contractors, etc.) and are authorized to continue functioning. Businesses authorized to remain operational can have difficulty conducting business if a major number of their workforce or supply chain providers become sick and are unable to report to work.

The Nieman guide from Harvard University suggests operational businesses consider the following:

1. Develop a chain of command structure to maintain business operations if individuals are unable to report to work
2. Develop and implement safety procedures and protective equipment for personnel in the workplace
3. Establish and maintain an effective internal and external communication process with current and accurate information
4. Provide necessary security to handle potentially stressful situations with employees and customers
5. Coordinate back-up or remote-access abilities to maintain company technology
6. Determine criticality of inventory items and coordinate delivery schedules with appropriate suppliers
7. Consult a business law attorney to remain aware of and comply with changing laws and government directives

Chapter 6   **Telecommuting**

Working from home

> **Disclaimer:** *The author of this Guide is <u>not</u> a trained or licensed attorney. Information shown in this chapter is written from a layman's view. It is based upon several years of business work experience and academic research. Nothing in this chapter is intended to be viewed as legal advice. It is simply sharing suggestions for a small business owner to consider during the planning and operation of their company.*

Telecommuting, or working from home can sound good on the surface, but employers need to be aware of liability concerns. There are many people who would argue working from home helps employee productivity and creativity through increased morale. It can save fuel, family time lost to commuting, and do good things for the environment.

It all sounds positive, but from a business perspective a small business owner should remain aware that he or she is required by laws and regulations to *carefully protect employees against liabilities* in their place of work whether it is a business office, or their own home. With the rise in telecommuting, courts have been treating the hazards an employee is exposed to while working from home in the same manner as the hazards they would be exposed to in their company workplace.

Examples:

State Compensation Insurance Fraud v. W.C.A.B./Kinnon, 45 Cal. Comp 253

A professor preparing class notes at home slipped on the papers he left lying on the floor and was injured. The court awarded him workers' compensation benefits.

Sandberg v. J.C.Penney, WCB No. 0702441, CA 140276

An employee working from home was injured when she tripped on her dog on the way to look for some company fabric samples in her garage. She was awarded workers' compensation benefits.

The concern

Owning and managing a business requires a more than average awareness of the law and its effect on the workplace. Even if a business owner registers for proper licenses with the government, operates with fairness and high ethical standards, and treats stakeholders, there are still liability issues to be aware of.

Home office liability

Telecommuting, or agreeing to have employees' conduct company business from their home involves the same safety and liability issues that apply when an employee is working in the company buildings. Before agreeing to have employees work from home, a business owner should familiarize themselves with the legal constraints that apply.

Safety standards and controls established by the Federal Occupational Safety and Health Act (OSHA) apply to all workers while they are conducting company business whether they are in company facilities or their homes (home based worksite).

> Home based worksite, as defined by OSHA Directive number CPL 202.125 is:
>
> The area of an employee's personal residence where the employee performs work of the employer. It is the location where the employee files, keyboards, does computer research, reads, or writes for the company. It may include equipment such as a telephone, facsimile machine, computer, scanner, copy machine, desk, and file cabinet.

OSHA may conduct inspections of home-based worksites if they receive a complaint or referral that indicates a violation of a safety or health standard exists that threatens physical harm, or that imminent danger exists.

Employers are responsible minimizing hazards caused by materials, equipment, or work processes which the employer provides or requires to be used in the employee's home.

This section only applies to business oriented Federal law. It does not include a discussion or state of local regulations that may override the federal law in a specific regional area.

Recommendation

Based upon apparent trends by the courts, employers should assume that the courts will treat hazards in the home in the same manner they would in the business workplace while the employee is "working." If the company does not have a clear and written policy for the employee working from home, they could be held responsible for an injury to an employee if they fell on some stairs while getting up in the middle of the night to get a drink and decided to check on their company email while they were up. They could be considered on work time since they were "doing company business."

A written telecommuting (working from home) company policy should be provided to each employee which clearly addresses:

- Expected work hours (while at home)
- Setting aside a specific area of the home for the employee to "work" in and if the employer feels it is necessary, the employer should be able to inspect the area for safety and ergonomic considerations
- Require the employee to take periodic breaks
- Have a clear job description for work to be done at home
- Be sure the employee understands telecommuting is a privilege, not a compensation benefit

Work from home insurance

According to AAA insurance, "more often than not, a standard homeowners insurance policy is adequate to keep a telecommuter well-covered. Having said that, there are special cases that present uncommon risks, which is why it is advisable to have employee's check with their insurance agent to let the employer and the company know whether they have any unexpected risks which should be covered."

Chapter 7 -- Employer-provided phones

According to the IRS Notice 2011-72, "...the IRS will consider all use of an employer-provided cell phone as a non-taxable fringe benefit so long as the cell phone is provided *primarily for non-compensatory business reasons.* The IRS provides the following explanations:

1. The term "cell phone" includes cellular telephones <u>or other similar</u> telecommunication equipment such as iPhones and Blackberries.

2. The notice eliminates the need for employers and/or employees to maintain records showing how much cell phone time is used for business and for personal reasons.

3. There will still be a requirement to have records indicating the cell phone is:

    a. Used to contact the employee at all times for work-related emergencies.
    b. Available for the employee to speak to clients at times when the employee is away from their workplace.
    c. Available for the employee to speak to clients in other time zones outside the employee's normal work hours.

A cell phone, according to the IRS is NOT a valid non-compensatory business expense if it:

1. Is provided as extra compensation for the employee.

2. Is provided to promote employee good will or improve relationships.

3. Is provided to attract a prospective employee (as part of their compensation).

Chapter 8 – Work-from-home legal concerns

Based upon recent court decisions, if an employee varies their normal route while going to or coming from work to provide an "incidental benefit" to the employer (pick something up, run a short errand, etc.), and the employee is involved in an accident, the employer can be held liable for the damages. The same employer liability can apply if an employee is involved in an accident in a company vehicle, even if they are doing personal business on non-work time.

Recommendation

To the extent possible, employers should not create a situation where an employee uses their personal vehicle during the workday, including commuting to and from work, to perform any work-related activities unless it is absolutely necessary.

Insurance companies offer car-pooling insurance to protect individual drivers and their employers.

Part three

Reopening a Business

People returning to the workplace will be looking for a safe, healthy, and modified setting – similar to what they remember from before the closure, customized to avoid risking future business closures.

This portion of the *Guide* provides some suggestions to help business owners consider issues they should address as they decide how to return to work in what will most likely be defined as a "new normal" operating environment.

Chapter 9 - Developing the reopening plan

Perception is everything in a reopened business

Each employee and customer will expect the company to understand their concerns about health and safety – and they will be looking for changes that have addressed their concerns.

Introduction

There is no printed script or design for a business *reopening plan*. The plan format the owner decides to use will become their own tool to help them think through issues they can expect to experience as they prepare to restart their business. The effort of *developing a reopening plan* will help the owner and staff be ready for a variety of problems, think of solutions in advance, and keep the company on track for a new beginning.

The reopening plan should be designed by the business owner and his or her support team. There is NO mandatory format or set requirement for topics to be included in their plan. It should be prepared in whatever way they are comfortable using for their company.

Possible steps to follow while planning for a reopening include:

Pause and Review

Begin planning the reopening process by taking some time to pause and think about the business – how was it performing before it closed? Should it go back to what it was, or could it improve by incorporating some changes during the restarting activities?

Areas to think about when envisioning the newly opened business include:

If the business was completely closed:

Why does the business exist?

What makes it stand out among competitors?

Did the company have a target market and was it reaching out to them?

Were customer relationships what they should be, or could there be changes made as the company reopens?

Were there enough repeat, or regular customers?

Were customers satisfied with the selection, quality, and price of products or services offered?

Should customer service or product quality be improved, or was it alright at the time of closure?

Were employees satisfied and motivated to remain with and support the company?

Was the facility adequate, efficiently arranged, capable of growth?

If the business was considered "essential" and able to stay open during the COVID-19 closure:

How well did it perform?

What worked and what could be improved?

Did people work from home or have on-line meetings?

How did productivity compare with pre-closure operations?

How was the communication equipment setup and maintained?

Were company records and customer information secure in the business office, in the communication process while on-line, and at the home or off-site location of the company employee?

Were there any "events" which might result in company losses of liability claims that could have been avoided if the employees were working in company facilities?

Did the business provide *hands off*, or *no personal contact* sales and service during the modified operation period?

Were customers and/or employees satisfied with the no contact operations?

Did any problems arise that could be resolved through improved *no contact* procedures?

Were there any problems with the *no contact* procedures that could not be taken care of without returning to former business processes.

Returning to work

Develop a phased approach for people returning to work, dependent upon their function and business requirements. Consider having some workers remain remote with others reporting to the company on different shifts of different days to avoid congestion in entry locations.

Include return to work schedules in the reopening plan as it is developed.

Health and Safety

Health and safety were the primary motivators for the government to require businesses to close and employees to stay home through lay off or in a work from home arrangement. Many people will be reluctant return to work for, or do business with a company that does not appear safe in terms of <u>visible housekeeping</u>, space between workstations, partitions (sneeze guards) designed to keep people separate while conducting business, etc.

Write a section of the *plan* explaining what the company will do to:

- provide enhanced health and safety awareness for the benefit of employees and customers

- train all employees in health, safety, and emergency response

- develop a schedule for regular deep cleaning and sanitizing of the workplace

Suggestions to consider:

- post entry instructions explaining company policy on social distancing

- provide sanitizing wipes at business entrance
- limit the number of customers allowed in the facility at the same time
- require masks for staff and customers
- between customer interchanges, wipe down (sterilize) all surfaces which are touched (e.g. counter tops, card readers, baskets/carts, etc.)
- staggered work times and/or days to minimize the number of employees in the building at the same time

Product delivery

Customers in many situations are becoming comfortable with no-contact takeout and product delivery. In support of the need to reduce potential spread of COPID-19, consider:

- accepting product orders remotely or by outside touch screen kiosk
- home delivery
- curb side delivery
- take out service from an inhouse counter requiring a printed or scanned pickup authorization

Cleaning, disinfecting, and sanitizing

The U.S. Center for Disease Control and Prevention (CDC) suggests "...non healthcare facilities such as schools, offices, daycare centers, businesses, etc. that do not house persons overnight" should *ensure workers are trained on the hazards of cleaning chemicals used in the workplace (reference OSHA Hazard Communication Standard 29-1910-1030)*

Suggestions to consider:

- develop and maintain a safety education program to educate staff and workers to recognize the symptoms of COVID-19 and provide instructions on what to do if they develop symptoms
- develop policies for worker protection and provide training to all cleaning staff on site prior to assigning cleaning tasks
- ensure workers are trained on the hazards of cleaning chemicals used in the workplace (reference OSHA Hazard Communication Standard 29-1910-1030)
- *after the close of business each day* clean and disinfect all areas such as offices, restrooms, common areas, shared electronic equipment (like tablets, touch screens, keyboards, remote controls, and

ATM machines) focusing on frequently touched surfaces.

For additional suggestions related to cleaning and disinfecting a workplace, see the following appendices:

<u>Appendix A – How to clean and disinfect</u> for CDC suggestions on disinfecting offices and office equipment.

<u>Appendix B – Office cleaning checklist</u> for use as a reminder of daily and weekly cleaning requirements.

Facility changes

Customers and employees are likely to expect businesses to change their facilities (aisles, furniture arrangements, product displays, waiting areas, etc.) to minimize person-to-person contact. Companies will be expected to be sanitized regularly, have hand disinfecting station available, and be arranged so customers and staff can pass each other with ample space (about 6 feet) between individuals.

After being through the COVID-19 no-contact period, customers will be comfortable with businesses using plexiglass protection around cashiers and counter workers, large meeting areas with less seating than before, one-way aisles, etc.

Before opening for business following the COVID-19 experience, business owners should consider the following changes to their facility to help them show customers and staff that they are proactively creating a healthy environment:

In addition to plexiglass barriers, access controls, signs addressing one-way aisles, etc. consider:

Entry/reception area

- remove magazines, pens, items likely to be handled by customers
- place hand sanitizer dispenser in clear view
- allow wide spacing between seating areas

Workstations

- if the office area included attached cubicles, remove chairs and monitors from every other one to discourage unauthorized use and maintain social distancing (store excess furniture to use as restrictions are removed)
- have all personal items removed from work surfaces at the end of each day to provide cleaning/sanitizing access

- install high partitions or shields between workstations, or reorient the workstation so employees do not face each other

Meeting/Training rooms

- place signs with maximum number of people allowed in each room and include a reminder of the need for social distancing (6 ft. space)
- place chairs with tables a social distance apart (store excess furniture to use as restrictions are removed)
- provide speakers, cameras, and monitors to support virtual meetings and training needs
- remove all files and work materials from work surfaces at the end of each day for cleaning and sanitizing
- establish a policy requiring employees to bring their own lunches and drinks rather than provide a coffee maker, birthday cakes, etc.

Marketing/advertising

Explain key elements of a marketing approach to reach out to former customers and attract new customers.

Provide an advertising overview explaining the use of flyers, signs, and use of social networking.

The following suggestions are intended to help company management and employees create a _startup attitude_ while generating more ideas on how to reconnect with former customers and find new ones:

Customer contact

- send reopening notices with a discount coupon to all customers on your records or reward program
- invite family and friends to your reopening
- send reopening notices to suppliers with gift cards they can pass on to potential customers (remember an increase in your business creates an increase in supplier business)
- check in with your Linkedin network and Facebook to let contacts and "friends" know you are reopening
- post signs on the building entrance announcing your reopening

- advertise the reopening in local newspapers with a discount coupon

Supplier relations

Explain how the company will work with former supply chain members to ensure adequate inventory during and after the reopening.

Coordinate inventory requirements to support the reopening schedule production needs.

Part four

Community Involvement

Chapter 10 – Working with the community

Work with the local Chamber of Commerce, business association, Economic Development Council, and other appropriate organizations to create a form of reopening fair or celebration for small businesses in the region.

Decide whether the reopening will be "soft" with minor publicity to former customers, or "hard" with fanfare to the general public.

Let the local business organizations know the business is reopening and tell them what changes have been incorporated to ensure public safety and give them the reopening date.

Send a news release to the local newspaper letting them know about the planned reopening and changes that will be seen by customers.

Ask the local business organizations if they can produce a recognizable sticker or decal for the business entrance identifying is as a COVID-19 sterilized zone, or some related message.

Bibliography

Business owner's tool kit, *Business templates,* Internet, (January 13, 2017).

Cleaning and disinfection for community facilities, (April 1, 2020), Center for Disease Control and Prevention.

Cleaning and disinfecting your facility. (April 14, 2929), Center for Disease Control and Prevention.

Fishman, S., J.D., *Checklist for closing your business,* NOLO legal guides, Internet.

How to announce you are liquidating and closing your business, Chron, Internet.

How to plan for workplace emergencies and evacuations, United States Department of Labor, Occupational Safety and Health Administration, Internet, (2001).

Kitsap County, Washington on-line *COVID-19 daily status report*, Internet.

Larkin, R., (2015), *Small business owner's desk reference,* Green Ivy Publishing, Oakbrook Terrace, IL.

Nieman guide to covering pandemic flue, Harvard University, (2009).

United States Small Business Administration Web site, Internet.

Appendix A – How to clean and disinfect

The information in this appendix is provided by the United States Center for Disease Control and Prevention.

<u>Hard (non-porous) surfaces</u>

- If surfaces are dirty, they should be cleaned using a detergent or soap and water prior to disinfection.

- For disinfection, most common EPA-registered household disinfectants should be effective.

- A list of products that are EPA-approved for use against the virus that causes COVID-19 is available on the Internet.

- Additionally, diluted household bleach (containing at least 1000ppm sodium hypochlorite) can be used if it is considered appropriate for the surface.

- Household bleach is effective as a disinfectant when mixed at 5 tablespoons (1/3) cup per gallon of water, or 4 teaspoons of bleach per quart of water.

NEVER MIX HOUSEHOLD BLEACH WITH AMMONIA OR ANY OTHER CLEANSER.

Soft (porous) surfaces

For soft surfaces such as carpeted floor, rugs, and drapes, remove visible contamination and clean with appropriate cleaners indicated for use on these surfaces

- If the items can be laundered, launder in accordance with manufacturer's instructions using the warmest appropriate water setting, then dry the items completely.

Electronics

For electronics such as tablets, touch screens, keyboards, remote controls, and ATM machines, remove visible contamination, then

- follow the manufacturer's instructions for all cleaning and disinfection products

- consider the use of wipeable covers for electronics

- if no manufacturer guidance is available, consider the use of alcohol-based wipes or sprays containing at least 70% alcohol to disinfect touch screens. Dry surfaces thoroughly to avoid pooling of liquids.

Linens, clothing, and other items that go in the laundry

In order to minimize the possibility of dispensing virus through the air, DO NOT SHAKE DIRTY LAUNDRY.

- Wash items as appropriate in accordance with the manufacturer's instructions. If possible, launder items using the warmest appropriate water setting for the items and dry items completely.
- Clean and disinfect hampers or other carts used for transporting laundry according to guidance above for hard or soft surfaces.

Appendix B – Office cleaning checklist

Regular office cleaning recommendations including steps to include sanitizing to prevent the spread of COVID-19:

<u>Every day</u>

Offices, cubicles and related work areas, lobby, conference rooms

Empty all trash receptacles and replace liners. Remove trash to a collection point.

Vacuum carpet

Clean, polish, and sanitize fountain/water cooler

Clean and sanitize all horizontal surfaces including desktops, files, windowsills, chairs, tables, pictures, and all furnishings (e.g. lamps, computer keyboards and telephones)

Mop hard surface floors with treated dust mop

Damp wipe and sanitize entry way, entrance glass, customer counters, cash register and related equipment, partition glass

Clean and sanitize all hand cleaner stations and refill sanitizer as needed

Restrooms

Stock towels, tissue, hand soap, sanitizer

Empty and sanitize trash receptacles

Clean, polish, and sanitize all mirrors and towel cabinet covers

Clean and sanitize all toilets and urinals including handles and fixtures as well as both sides of toilet seats

Scour and sanitize all sinks and basins

Mop and rinse restroom floors using disinfectant

Breakroom(s)

Empty all trash receptacles and replace liners. Remove trash to a collection point.

Clean and sanitize all sinks, food preparation locations, countertops, drawers and drawer handles, and nearby walls

Mop and rinse hard surface floors using disinfectant

Vacuum carpet

Damp wipe and sanitize entry way, entry doors, railings, customer counters, cash register and related equipment, partition glass

Clean and sanitize all hand cleaner stations and refill sanitizer as needed

Inspect and remove trash, leaves, etc. from building entrance area

ABOUT THE AUTHOR

Richard Larkin, M.B.A., Ed.D. has been a Counselor and Certified Mentor with the U.S. Small Business Administration. His working career includes owning and managing a wide range of production and retail companies. He has been a professor with several colleges and universities located in Washington, Maryland, and Germany. Richard lives in Washington State with his wife, their cat, and neighboring deer.